Functional-ish

Real Life Hacks From A Messy Mom
Just Trying to Keep the Remote Where It Belongs

by Genevieve C. West

Lulu Press Inc

Copyright © 2025 Genevieve C. West

All Rights Reserved

Book design by Genevieve C. West

e-book ISBN: 978-1-300-22561-4

Print ISBN: 978-1-300-22551-5

Imprint: Lulu.com

Published by Lulu Press Inc.

627 Davis Dr, Ste 300, Morrisville, NC 27560, US

This book is dedicated to all the mamas who can't figure out how other people seem to always have their house in order and life together.

And to my delightful spawn who suffer through these experiments with me.

I love you guys.

Table of Contents

QuickStart Guide: Overwhelmed? Start Here.	7
Welcome to My Hot Mess Life	10
Body Doubling and Manga Magic	13
Mismatched Socks and Other Freedoms	16
Entryway Peace Treaties	19
The Dish Revolution	22
One Bathroom, Six People	25
Everything Needs a Home	29
Seasons Change—So Should Your Systems	34
Labels Won't Save You, But They Sure Help	37
"Get-Your-Butt-in-Gear" Cheat Sheet	40
When You Need a Reset Button (Because You're Not a Failure, You're Just Fried)	42
Bonus Tid Bits For Real Life Sanity	48
Reader Reflection Page	49
Permission Slips	50
Hot Mess Brain Hack: Why Pen & Paper Checklists Actually Work	51
Hot Mess Hit List: Common Chaos Zones to Conquer	52
Books That Sparked Joy, Sanity, or Self-Acceptance	54
Author Bio	56

"Housework can't kill you, but why take a chance?"

— Phyllis Diller

QuickStart Guide:
Overwhelmed? Start Here.

Feeling like your house is eating you alive? Deep breath. You don't need to do everything at once. You don't even need to finish this book. Just pick one of these to try this week:

- Laundry Two-Basket System: One basket for clean, one for dirty. No sorting. No matching. Zero shame.

- Entryway Drop Zones: Assign one zone per kid. NOTHING gets past the entryway.

- Label Something. Anything. Masking tape + Sharpie = instant order. Label where the remote really lives.

- Set Up One Trash Can Where You Actually Need It: Couch corner? Kid's desk? You already know where the trash lands.

- Start a Catch-All Basket for Each Person: When in doubt, toss it in their bin.

Pick one. Try it. If it helps? Celebrate. If not? Toss it and try the next thing. This is your rhythm now.

Hot Mess Household Hacks That Work For Us

- **Body Doubling Is Magic**

Cleaning sucks less when we do it together, even if we're not doing the same task. Proximity = productivity.

- **Two-Basket Laundry System**

One for dirty, one for clean. No sorting. Everyone does their own laundry. Mismatched socks are a lifestyle.

- **Entryway Rule: Stop & Drop**

Nothing enters the house beyond the entryway. Everyone has their own zone. Donate bin lives by the door.

- **Compostable Dishes Saved My Sanity**

Four meals a day during COVID = dish overload. Compostable plates + green bin = peace. Never looked back.

- **Hygiene Stations Outside the Bathroom**

Toothbrushes, makeup, hair care, everything that doesn't need privacy lives outside the bathroom now.

- **Everything Needs a Home (Even if It's Weird)**

Follow the "desire path." If it always ends up there, that's where it belongs. Label it. Tray it. Own it.

- **Trash Cans Everywhere**

One per bedroom, desk, sofa side, and entryway. Yes, it's extra. Yes, it works.

- **Catch-All Baskets**

Each person has a basket under their eating spot. Found your kid's weird rock collection? Toss it in their bin.

- Seasonal Stuff Gets Its Own Bin

Snow gear, Halloween chaos, pool floaties, all live in clear, labeled bins. No more seasonal scavenger hunts.

- Flexible Systems Win

What worked last year may not work now, and that's okay. Peel off the masking tape, relabel, and pivot.

- Charging Cords Are Everywhere

Forget the "one perfect charging station." Every zone gets a charger. No more "who stole my cord?" fights.

- Perfection Is a Lie

Label the chaos. Love the mess. Adapt constantly. You're not failing, you're evolving.

Welcome to My Hot Mess Life

"You don't have to be everything to everyone."

— Brené Brown

I am not what you'd call a "together" person. I'm more of a "held together with caffeine, humor, and misplaced phone chargers" kind of person. I'm an unmotivated ADHD mom with a healthy splash of anxiety, a side of depression, and four gloriously feral children who would all rather be building cardboard rollercoasters in the living room or painting the bunny neon pink than, say, putting their socks in a drawer.

Cleaning? Organizing? Folding anything? Yeah… no. Not unless it's origami and even then, only if it's part of an art project.

Just so we're clear, this is so NOT a Pinterest-perfect household. There are no chalkboard chore charts here, no soothing neutrals, no "blessed" signs hanging in the entryway (unless they're ironic). This is not a minimalist, color-coordinated, Instagrammable dream home. This is barely controlled chaos, and that's on a good day.

But somehow, through the wild mess of daily life, we've created a system that works. Not perfectly, not even consistently, but good enough to keep us afloat. And when you're parenting through ADHD, anxiety, and depression? "Good enough" is a freaking win.

This little book isn't going to guilt you into decluttering or tell you your clutter is a reflection of your inner demons. Nope! This is about the real kind of organizing. The kind that takes years of experimenting and pouring over ADHD Mom blogs for hacks that have worked for others. The kind that says, "What if we just had a trash can where everyone already throws their wrappers instead of yelling at them to use the one across the room?" Revolutionary.

It's about masking tape labels, paper plates, and enough baskets to contain (some of) the madness. It's about finding ways to keep things running just enough so we don't all spiral into a doom pit of laundry and misplaced library books. (There's a bin labeled "Library Books" next to the sofa, along with the library cards. No new books are checked out until the last batch are returned. You're welcome.)

So if you're tired of "perfect mom" energy and need some real-talk hacks from someone who absolutely does not have her life together, pull up a floor cushion and stay awhile. This is a judgment-free zone, with snacks.

Welcome to my hot mess life.

Reality Check

What part of your own home or routine feels the most "hot mess" right now—and how can you give yourself a little more grace in that area?

Have you been holding yourself to someone else's standard of "together"?

If you stopped aiming for perfect and started aiming for peace, what would change?

Tiny Win Challenge

Clear one surface in your home that's been stressing you out.

Just one. A nightstand, a bathroom counter, the black hole of doom that is your kitchen island. Toss the trash, relocate the clutter, give it five minutes of love—and step back to admire your small but mighty victory.

Body Doubling and Manga Magic

"There is no such thing as failure. You either succeed or you learn."

— Oprah Winfrey

The Joy (and Comic Relief) of Tidying Up

Once upon a meltdown, one of those "I'm going to throw everything we own into a dumpster and start over" kind of meltdowns, I impulse bought my kids the manga version of Marie Kondo's The Life Changing Magic of Tidying Up.

Why the manga? Other than because my kids only actually enjoy reading manga? Because regular Marie felt a little too put-together and judgmental for my mental state. But manga Marie? She came with sparkles, anime eyes, and way less pressure. We were sold.

The kids read it cover to cover, laughing at the overreactions and dramatic fold scenes, but somewhere in the middle of all that chaos and comic relief, a little lightbulb went off. Maybe we could tidy up. Maybe we just needed to do it *our* way—loud, weird, and together.

That's where body doubling came in.

If you're unfamiliar, body doubling is basically ADHD life support. It's when you do a task while someone else is in the room, even if they're doing something completely different. For ADHD brains, the mere presence of another human doing anything remotely productive is a weird kind of magic. Suddenly, folding socks doesn't feel so isolating. Taking out the trash isn't so overwhelming. It's like peer pressure, but wholesome.

So we started doing this as a family. Not "group chore time" in the traditional sense (because that sounds awful), but more like "everyone pick your personal mess and deal with it while we vibe in the same room." Sometimes we're actually cleaning. Sometimes one kid is drawing, another is picking up Legos, I'm sorting papers, and someone is laying on the floor pretending to be productive. That still counts. Being near each other helps.

It's less about the chore and more about the energy. We crank up music, share space, and keep each other from doom spiraling. When one of us runs out of motivation, someone else is usually just hitting their stride. We take turns having energy, and we ride each other's waves.

We talk, we joke, we move around, and before we know it, the house is 15% less terrifying. Which, in this household, is a massive win.

It's also taught us that organizing doesn't have to look like those Instagram reels with beige bins and flower arrangements on every shelf. It can be mismatched, chaotic, loud, and still feel magically manageable. That's what manga Marie gave us: permission to laugh while we declutter and be our messy selves in the process.

Because sometimes all you need is a little anime inspiration, a trash bag, and someone nearby folding laundry while you purge the junk drawer. Welcome to body doubling: the ADHD mom's secret weapon.

Reality Check

- Are you expecting yourself (or your kids) to clean in total isolation?

- Do you feel stuck because you think you need motivation before starting—when maybe what you actually need is company?

- Who could you body double with this week? (Spouse, kid, friend on FaceTime, imaginary anime cleaning squad...)

Tiny Win Challenge

Grab someone—anyone—and clean for 10 minutes in the same room.

Don't overthink it. You can both do different things. Just being near each other helps. No pressure to finish—just move some energy together and see what happens.

Mismatched Socks and Other Freedoms

"My idea of housework is to sweep the room with a glance."

— Erma Bombeck

No Sorting, No Matching, No Problem

Laundry in this house isn't a team sport, it's a survival strategy. And we're all just trying to make it to next week with clean underwear. It's about self-preservation. Everyone's got their own system, and honestly? That's what keeps us alive.

Which is why, in my infinite wisdom (and infinite overwhelm), I made the executive decision that everyone handles their own laundry. Yes, even the youngest (often with help and reminders). If you can get glitter into your socks, you can learn how to get it back out.

Here's our system: two laundry baskets per person. One for dirty, one for clean. That's it. That's the magic. The whole "fold and put away immediately" fantasy? Yeah, that's not happening. Life gets busy, neurodivergent brains get distracted, and sometimes that clean basket becomes a portable dresser for a solid week. Or two. We don't judge.

Now, each kid has developed their own laundry personality:

- One kid folds everything like they work retail. I don't know where they got that from. Definitely not me. Maybe they were swapped at birth.

- One refuses to use drawers at all and proudly rocks the Two Basket Life: one for clean, one for dirty, and good vibes only in between.

- And then there's the one who takes after me: tosses vaguely clean clothes into vaguely correct drawers, organized mostly by vibes and desperation.

And socks? Oh honey. Socks are an entire saga.

Each kid has a mesh sock bag next to where their shoes come off, because if stinky socks don't go somewhere, they go everywhere.

One of my children (you know who you are) takes the time to safety pin their socks together before putting them in their mesh bag. I love them, but that level of discipline is suspicious. The rest of us? We just toss our socks in the bag and pray to the laundry gods.

Each kid tosses their personal stink-bomb mesh bag into the wash with their clothes. Then they immediately replace it with a backup mesh bag, because stinky sock disposal waits for no one. It's a flawless system. Okay, not flawless. But functional. And that's what we aim for.

Also, each person gets two towels. That's it. Two. When you wash your clothes, you wash your towel. It's part of the deal. I do keep a stash of "emergency towels" for summer shenanigans and spilled smoothies, but my personal goal in life is to never again hear someone yell, "Mom! Are there any clean towels?!"

Because yes, there are clean towels. And yes, I am a genius. A tired, under-caffeinated, slightly chaotic genius with a laundry system that mostly works.

If this chapter gave you any revolutionary ideas, feel free to run with them. Or don't. Just promise me you'll stop matching socks unless it genuinely sparks joy.

Reality Check

- Are you still trying to be the Laundry Martyr™ for the whole house?

- Are you clinging to laundry systems that worked before kids, or before you had a whole life to manage?

- Is matching socks worth the rage it sparks? (Spoiler: It's not.)

Tiny Win Challenge

Give each person in your house a second laundry basket or bag—right now.

Label it "clean" or "dirty," and let that be their new system. No sorting. No matching. No shame. Just simplified laundry and fewer excuses.

Entryway Peace Treaties

"Don't try to win over the haters; you're not the jackass whisperer."

— Brené Brown

Preventing Sibling Wars

I have one rule that holds the entire fabric of my household together: NOTHING COMES INTO THE HOUSE AFTER THE ENTRYWAY.

That's it. That's the law. That's my religion.

This rule isn't just about the kids knowing where their cleats and jackets are, it's about *my* survival. If I don't stop at the door and unload my life, everything implodes within minutes. I'm talking keys in the fridge. Sunglasses on a cereal box. Purse in the toy box. Phone? On silent. Last seen on top of the bathroom trash can. Jacket? Crumpled behind the sofa, forgotten until I'm late and freezing.

So I trained myself like a Pavlovian house elf:

- Keys and sunglasses go in the bowl.
- Purse and jacket get hung up.
- Shoes hit the bottom shelf.
- House shoes go on.

And only then am I allowed to proceed into the house like a civilized adult (or whatever approximation of one I'm capable of being that day).

If I don't follow the ritual, the consequences are swift and ridiculous. I end up crying over missing earbuds and retracing my steps like a lost Victorian ghost. So now I don't mess around. I stop, I strip, I switch modes. Entryway is the decompression chamber between public me and sofa me.

For the kids, I carved out the same kind of magic: their own designated drop zones, socially distanced six feet apart, like it's a sneaker pandemic. No overlap. No encroachment. This wasn't some cute Pinterest idea. It was forged in the fires of sibling warfare. You haven't seen true rage until a 9-year-old accuses her sister of touching her sparkly high-tops.

Coats, shoes, backpacks, skateboards, helmets, everything gets parked in their personal zone. The spacing is deliberate. Strategic. Ruthless. I don't care if it wrecks the aesthetic. I care about peace in the kingdom. And in this house, sibling spillage is forbidden.

This system isn't cute. It's not color-coded. But it keeps us sane. And most importantly, it keeps the morning chaos contained to one part of the house.

The living room is not a shoe graveyard. The hallway is not a lost-and-found. The entryway is our battlefield-turned-truce zone, and honestly, we've never been more peaceful.

And because I like to strike while the motivation iron is hot (which, let's be honest, is rare and fleeting), we have a permanent donate bin right by the door. It's a regular old bin with a trash bag liner, but it's sacred. The second something doesn't fit, feel good, or get used? Into the bin it goes. Toys, games, clothes, shoes, if you don't want it, we're not keeping it. We don't debate it. We don't hold a family vote. We just let it go.

Because if I have to trip over the same pair of too-small soccer cleats one more time, I will absolutely burn them in front of God and everyone.

Reality Check

- Are you letting backpacks, shoes, and mystery items creep past your entryway and take over your house?
- Do your kids know where their stuff actually goes—or are you just hoping they figure it out telepathically?
- Is the entryway system working, or is it secretly a chaos pile in disguise?

Tiny Win Challenge

Create or reclaim one "drop zone" near your entryway.

Clear the space. Assign it to one person. Add a bin, hook, crate, or label—whatever works. Make it unmistakably theirs. Then stand back and admire the lack of shoe sprawl.

The Dishes Revolution

"I hate housework. You make the beds, you do the dishes—and six months later, you have to start all over again."

— Joan Rivers

How COVID Broke My Dishwashing Will to Live

Let's set the scene: It's the peak of the pandemic. We're all stuck inside, schools are closed, the world is weird, and I'm making four full meals a day plus snacks for a family of six. Every. Single. Day.

Do you know what happens when six people eat that much?

A mountain of dishes.

Not a metaphorical mountain. A literal ceramic Everest rising out of my sink, threatening to collapse and bury me alive in a landslide of ramen bowls and mismatched spoons.

I snapped. I wanted to smash every dish we owned (and okay, a few did meet an untimely end during that period). So I did what any exhausted, rage-washing ADHD mom would do:

I ordered bulk compostable everything.

Plates. Cups. Bowls. Ramen bowls. Forks. Spoons. Even the fancy ones for soup. It felt like prepper-level brilliance. It wasn't just laziness, it was a strategic move to preserve my mental health and my will to live.

But the best part? We trained the kids to use the green compost bin. That was the deal. If we're gonna go full disposable, we're going to do it responsibly. It took a few "NO,

NOT THE REGULAR TRASH" reminders, but they caught on fast. And the sheer joy of tossing your plate away after dinner instead of scraping, rinsing, and stacking? Chef's kiss.

After COVID, everyone asked me, "So... are you going back to real dishes now?"

Absolutely not. I'd rather fight a raccoon than go back to washing 40 pieces of tableware a day. This system works. The Earth can forgive me—I'm using compostables.

But we didn't stop there. One day, during a "come to Jesus" family meeting about kitchen chores, we had a breakthrough. Turns out, two of my kids hate loading the dishwasher, and the other two (myself included) loathe unloading it. Like, soul-deep resentment.

So we made teams: The Loaders vs. The Unloaders. Now we rotate between teams and everyone knows what part of the job is theirs. No more chore confusion. No more emotional breakdowns over a rogue spatula. Just clear roles and fewer fights.

Oh, and water cups? Gone. We now have coasters on the kitchen counter with each person's name written in Sharpie. That's where your water bottle lives. No more "which cup is mine?" or 900 cups in the sink by noon.

We also eat at the counter. Always. Each kid has their designated seat and is responsible for keeping their personal food zone clean. And yes, some of us (you know who you are) treat the table like a secondary plate. So this rule helps keep things fair. You make the mess, you wipe it up.

These aren't glamorous systems. No stainless steel bento boxes. No inspirational dinnerware. Just function over fantasy, and a mom who no longer cries into her sponge.

Reality Check

- Are dishes the hill you're quietly dying on every single day?
- Do you keep trying to be eco-perfect at the cost of your sanity?
- Is your dishwashing "system" just a polite way of saying "emotional minefield"?

Tiny Win Challenge

Buy a pack of compostable or paper plates and give yourself a break.

Use them for one meal—or one whole day—and see how it feels to not be buried in the sink. Bonus points if you train your crew to toss them in the right bin.

One Bathroom, Six People

"Having a family is like having a bowling alley installed in your brain."

— Martin Mull

Let's talk about a special kind of chaos: six humans. One bathroom.

If you've never had to brush your teeth while someone else is trying to make a stinky in peace, count your blessings. In this house, we've mastered the delicate dance of urgency vs. dignity.

For an embarrassing amount of time, I thought the problem was that our bathroom was too small. Or that we needed better storage solutions. Or chore charts. Or divine intervention.

Nope.

The actual problem was this: I was trying to cram ALL the things that could possibly be related to grooming, hygiene, or basic human upkeep into the ONE room in the house that locks from the inside.

Spoiler alert: not everything needs to be in the bathroom!

Wild concept. Took me way too long to get there.

So I made some changes that saved our mornings, and probably our family's sanity.

Step one: drawer stations OUTSIDE the bathroom.

Hairbrushes, deodorant, scrunchies, bobby pins, band-aids, tweezers, sunscreen, all got evicted. I set up small drawer towers and organizers right outside the bathroom and labeled them like a woman on the brink.

The effect was instant. Fewer fights. Fewer tears. Fewer hallway traffic jams with someone screaming, "I just need to get my HAIR GEL!"

Step two: relocate the dental drama.

Toothbrushes and toothpaste now live by the kitchen sink. You know what else lives there? Dental floss, mouthwash, and the occasional rogue retainer. It's convenient, no one hogs the bathroom while brushing their teeth, and we've saved more than one outfit from getting splashed by a rogue rinse-and-spit.

Step three: build a humidity-proof glam station.

Makeup does not belong in a steamy bathroom. Period. We now have a lighted mirror in the hallway and a small vanity tray setup so anyone who wants to beat their face to perfection can do so without sweating off the results.

It can look like a backstage dressing room exploded next to the coat closet, but at least we're not fighting over a fogged-up mirror and mascara streaks.

Bonus: trays are everything.

Bottles of lotion and hair spray no longer live in a lawless pile on the counter. Instead, they live in trays—which magically makes the chaos feel intentional. Somehow, placing 12 half-used products inside a rectangle makes them feel classy. Do I understand the science? No. Do I accept the magic? Absolutely.

Is it still a little chaotic? Yes. Do we still have traffic jams and "I NEED TO PEE AND THEY'RE IN THE SHOWER" emergencies? Obviously. But it's no longer a total war zone.

Because when you only have one bathroom and a whole house full of people, the trick isn't getting more space. The trick is getting smart with the space you've got, and evicting everything that doesn't truly belong.

One bathroom. Six people. Still standing.

Barely.

Reality Check

- Are you treating your one bathroom like it's supposed to serve six full routines, six hygiene preferences, and six stress levels… all at once?
- Is it actually a storage problem—or a location problem?
- How much stuff in your bathroom could live somewhere else and make everyone's life easier?

Tiny Win Challenge

Move one non-essential category out of the bathroom.

Hair stuff, toothbrushes, makeup, first aid—pick one and relocate it to a drawer, bin, or tray outside the bathroom. Congestion cleared. Crisis averted.

Everything Needs a Home

"Perfectionism is a 200-pound shield that we lug around thinking it will protect us..."

— Brené Brown

Desire Paths, Sharpies, and Why Cute Baskets Don't Always Win

Let me hit you with a universal truth: if something doesn't have a home, it will always be out of place. Always. No matter how many lectures you give, chore charts you print, or Pinterest boards you pin.

But here's the kicker: it can't just *have* a home. That home has to make sense. It has to be just as easy to put the thing away as it is to toss it somewhere random. I'm going to say that again, because it's become our household mantra:

It has to be just as easy to put it away as it is to not put it away.

If your hand naturally always wants to drop your lotion on the windowsill instead of inside a cabinet? Congratulations, that's the lotion's new home now. Put it on a tray, give it dignity, and move on.

This philosophy is called following the desire path, following the way humans naturally prefer, rather than the path humans artificially create. So put things where they always land, not where the Ideal Organized Pinterest Mom says they should go.

Take the remote, for example. You know that cute basket you put on the coffee table with hopes and dreams? Yeah, the remote never lives there. It lives on the back of the couch. So that's where I gave it a basket and a label, because I believe in accepting reality and adjusting accordingly.

Enter: The Label Life

I am not ashamed to say that masking tape and Sharpie are my family's design aesthetic. Everything is labeled, and more importantly, everything is relabel-able. If something stops working, we peel, re-stick, and rename. Because life is seasonal. Interests change. Routines shift. What worked last spring might be chaos this fall.

Trash Cans Everywhere

We do not believe in "one trash can per house" minimalism. We are a neurospicy household, and that means trash cans live where the trash happens:

- One next to every bed
- One at each desk
- One on each side of the living room sofa
- One by the command center
- One by the front door

Yes, it's a lot. But yes, it keeps us clean(ish). When the trash can is always within arm's reach, there are fewer wrappers under the sofa cushions and less passive-aggressive muttering from me at 11pm.

Catch-All Baskets: The Lost & Found of Sanity

Each person has a catch-all basket underneath their eating area. This is where all the random things go. Legos, chapsticks, Pokémon cards, emotional support rubber bands, all without interrupting someone's flow. No more tossing stuff on their beds or chasing them down mid-task. It goes in the basket, and when the basket is full (or overflowing like a symbolic cry for help), they deal with it.

Eventually.

With prompting.

Possibly bribes.

Jars, Bowls, and Pen Holders Galore

I noticed hair ties always ended up in the same spot, so I put a pretty jar there. Magically, now they don't end up in the vacuum.

Every surface that tends to collect clutter now has a bowl or basket to catch it.

Anywhere we often write? A pen holder lives there. Because I got tired of digging up 50 pencils from between couch cushions like I was on a sad archaeological dig. I always need scissors when I'm on the sofa, but they never make it back to their shelf. Now some scissors also live in the pen holder by the sofa.

Charger Chaos, Solved

My dream of a single, sleek charging station is just that—a dream. In reality, I want to charge my phone anywhere it hits 20%. So now we have chargers permanently placed:

- By each bed
- At every desk
- In the kitchen
- Two on the living room sofa

No more disappearing chargers. No more "who stole my cord?" arguments. Just energy flowing and devices staying alive. It's beautiful.

At the end of the day, this system isn't about being hyper-organized, it's about being realistic. About watching how your family actually lives and building the house around that, not against it.

Because in this house? Everything has a home. And if it doesn't... well, it better find one fast or it's going in the donation bin after I trip over it.

Of course, the easiest way to organize something is to not have to organize it at all. Some things don't need a home, they need an exit.

With so many people under one roof, I've learned the hard way: I don't need more bins or shelves or hooks.

I need less stuff to organize.

These days, I'm absolutely brutal about what stays. Clothes with stains? Tossed. Ripped, stretched-out, threadbare? Thank you for your service—off you go.

Once upon a time, I was the mom who lovingly mended holes in jeans and glued googly eyes back onto broken toys. Now? Unless it's truly loved or still functional, I don't waste the energy. It's not cold-hearted—it's growth. I've changed. My time, space, and sanity are worth more than a pile of "maybe I'll fix this someday."

I no longer hold onto things just because they used to be useful. If it's not serving us right now, it's out.

Because honestly? I've got better things to do than organize a graveyard of half-broken intentions.

Reality Check

- Are you constantly picking up the same item over and over... because it doesn't actually have a home?
- Are you organizing based on what looks good—or where things naturally land?
- Are your "systems" secretly just wishful thinking in cute baskets?

Tiny Win Challenge

Pick one item that's always out of place—and give it a real home.

Use a tray, a bowl, a label, a bin, or even a shoebox. Bonus points if it follows the "desire path" (aka where your family actually puts it). Order, restored.

Seasons Change—So Should Your Systems

"What if I told you that you could mess up, fall apart, start late, or be imperfect... and still be worthy of love and respect?"

— Glennon Doyle

Why This System Works (Until It Doesn't)

Here's the thing about life—especially life with ADHD, kids, emotions, moods, and ever-shifting chaos: it's not static. So our systems? They shouldn't be either.

The biggest (and most freeing) lesson I've learned is this:

Systems are allowed to evolve.

What worked last year might suck this year. What felt like the holy grail of organization might now feel like a confusing mess that makes your brain twitch. That's not failure, that's life!

We used to have one big unorganized shelf for all the seasonal stuff. That turned into an annual scavenger hunt when the first snow fell or the outdoor pools opened back up. So now? Clear, labeled bins.

One for costumes.

One for snow gear.

One for rain gear.

One for "summer fun" (aka swimsuits, goggles, deflated donuts).

Each bin is labeled in big Sharpie letters, and when the season is over, we chuck everything in its bin and shove it in the closet like emotional baggage. It's not fancy, but it's functional, and it keeps the seasonal panic attacks to a minimum.

And when we inevitably realize that a "perfect system" no longer works? We pivot. No guilt. No shame. Just peel off the masking tape, slap on a new label, and try again.

Because this house doesn't run on rigidity, it runs on rhythm. And like any good rhythm, it's allowed to change tempo. We adapt based on interests, ages, needs, and energy levels. Some years, the kids are into sports. Other years, it's all Legos and cosplay. One month, we're all about painting and puzzles. The next? Chaos and cardboard forts.

And the systems we build have to keep up.

That's why everything in this house is modular, label-able, movable, and absolutely up for renegotiation. We're not running a museum. We're building a home that bends and flexes and breathes along with us.

So if something worked beautifully last year and now it just makes you want to scream into a pillow, ditch it. Experiment! Adjust. Reconfigure. Flow.

Because rhythm beats rigor, every single time.

Reality Check

- Are you still using a system that worked last year but now feels like trying to wear jeans from high school?
- Are you resisting change because you think pivoting means failure?
- Are your closets or routines full of "used to work" energy that's just taking up space now?

Tiny Win Challenge

Choose one system, space, or routine that's not working—and give yourself permission to change it.

Ditch the chore chart that no one follows. Swap bins. Relabel something. Let go of what used to fit and build what works right now.

Labels Won't Save You, But They Sure Help

"No one can make you feel inferior without your consent."

— Eleanor Roosevelt

Anyone who knows me will agree—I do not have my life together.

Not a little. Not even close. I forget appointments. I burn dinner while answering emails. I've definitely poured coffee into a cereal bowl because my brain glitched mid-task. This is not a household of perfection. This is a household of improvisation, resilience, and chaotically creative survival.

But you know what I do have? Systems. Not fancy ones. Not Instagrammable ones. But real, lived-in, scribbled-on-with-a-Sharpie systems that work for us. Systems that change when we change. Systems that leave room for growth, mess, mistakes, and magic.

Because this isn't about having it all together. This is about staying afloat *together*.

It's about recognizing when something isn't working and being brave enough to throw it out and try something new, even if it's just trading cute bins for trays or labeling a remote's new "home" on the back of the couch.

It's about giving yourself permission to build a life that fits your rhythm, not someone else's rules.

If even one of these weird little hacks helps another overwhelmed, exhausted, beautifully imperfect mom breathe a little easier? Then this book did its job.

Because at the end of the day, we're all just trying to create a home where our kids can be wild and wonderful, and we can find the remote when we need it.

So label your chaos.

Love your mess.

And never, ever underestimate the power of masking tape.

You've got this.

Reality Check

- Are you expecting your family to magically know where things go without ever telling or showing them?

- Are your labels outdated, ignored, or nonexistent—and you're still wondering why the system's falling apart?

- Have you outgrown a setup but haven't given yourself permission to change it?

Tiny Win Challenge

Label (or relabel) one thing that causes daily confusion.

Use masking tape and a Sharpie. Don't wait for the label maker. Don't overthink the font. Just make it clear and make it work. Clarity = sanity.

"Get-Your-Butt-in-Gear" Cheat Sheet

Hot Mess Momentum: Quick Tricks to Get Moving When You'd Rather Rot

Because no, motivation doesn't come first. Action comes first, and sometimes it needs a little shove.

Give Yourself a Pep Talk (Out Loud. Yes, Out Loud.)

Say it in the mirror. Say it while you pee. Say it while you look at your clutter pile:

"I don't have to do it all. I just have to do *something*."

"I can handle 10 minutes of anything."

"Hot mess? Maybe. Capable hot mess? Absolutely."

Play the Music You Used to Pregame To

Channel your pre-mom club era. Beyoncé, Missy Elliott, Rage Against the Machine, whatever made you feel like a badass.

This is not dishwashing music. This is main character energy music.

Set a 15-Minute Timer and Race Yourself

You'll be shocked what gets done under time pressure. Don't clean perfectly, just move fast and don't stop.

Invite a Friend Over (Even If They Just Sit There)

Nothing lights a fire under your butt like knowing someone's about to see your chaos.

Worst case: they body double.

Best case: they help.

Either way: progress.

Use the "One Song, One Surface" Rule

Put on one song. Clean one surface. That's it. When the song ends, you're done, or maybe you're in the groove and keep going. Either way, it counts.

Dress Like You're Filming a Cleaning Montage

Put on a cute hoodie, your favorite messy bun, or a ridiculous apron. When you look the part, you play the part.

Light a Candle, Turn on a Lamp, Open a Window

A sensory shift can cue your brain that something new is starting. It doesn't have to be deep, it just has to be different.

When You Need a Reset Button

(Because You're Not a Failure, You're Just Fried)

Sometimes, it's not about a new system.

Sometimes, it's not about a cute label, or a new basket, or picking one small surface to clean.

Sometimes, you've hit the wall. You've stared at the mess so long that it's just background noise, and no amount of Tiny Win Challenges will pull you out of the fog.

That's when it's time to hit the Reset Button, and no, that doesn't mean you're weak or lazy or failing. It means you're human.

Here's how to ask for help when the house feels like a disaster zone and you're just trying not to cry over spilled Goldfish crackers.

Phone a Friend (Yes, Really)

Ask someone you trust to come over, not to judge or fix, just to body double while you reset one area. Say:

"I'm overwhelmed and stuck. Can you sit with me while I try to tackle one space?"

Sometimes just having another person nearby will shake loose the shame and get you moving.

Hire Help Without Guilt

If you can afford it, hire a cleaner or organizer for a deep reset. Look for someone who specializes in ADHD, hoarding, or chronic disorganization, not just "speed cleaners."

Say this when calling:

"I'm looking for help with a non-judgmental deep clean. I have ADHD and I'm overwhelmed by clutter. Do you have experience with that?"

You're not hiring someone because you're lazy. You're hiring them because you're smart enough to ask for support when you need it most.

How to Find Professional Help That Gets It

Not all cleaners or organizers are created equal, and when you're dealing with ADHD, depression, executive dysfunction, or hoarding, you need someone who understands that this isn't just mess, it's mental load.

Here's how to find help without inviting judgment into your home:

Use the Right Search Terms

When looking online, search for things like:

- "ADHD-friendly house cleaning services near me"
- "Organizers for chronic disorganization"
- "Compassionate cleaning for hoarding"

- "Non-judgmental home reset help"

- "Body doubling cleaning help + [your city]"

- "Professional organizer for neurodivergent families"

These keywords can help filter out the high-pressure, Pinterest-perfect types.

Search These Trusted Sites

- NAPO (National Association of Productivity & Organizing Professionals)

- Click "Find a Pro" and filter by specialties like ADHD or mental health support.

- ICD (Institute for Challenging Disorganization)

- These pros are literally trained to help people who feel buried in clutter. Look for certifications in Chronic Disorganization or Hoarding.

- TaskRabbit or Care.com

- You can find independent cleaners or organizers and screen for gentle, neurodivergent-aware personalities.

- Local Facebook Groups or Buy Nothing Groups

- Ask: "Does anyone know of a cleaner or organizer who works well with ADHD or overwhelmed moms?" You'll be shocked how often someone knows someone perfect.

What to Say When Reaching Out

Not sure how to ask? Try this script:

"Hi! I'm looking for cleaning or organizing support, but I want to be up front, I have ADHD and struggle with executive function. I'm not looking for judgment or perfection, just compassionate help getting things functional again. Do you have experience working with clients like that?"

Anyone worth hiring will say "Absolutely, no problem."

Anyone who sounds condescending or rigid? Hard pass.

Use a "Disaster Relief" Mentality

Treat your home like it just survived a storm, because emotionally, it did.

Focus on function, not perfection:

- Clear one path to the bed
- Make one surface usable
- Throw out the trash, don't sort it

You can organize later. Right now, your job is to make it livable again.

Try a Local Resource

Depending on where you live, you might find:

- ADHD-informed cleaning services
- Professional organizers who get it (look for NAPO or ICD certification)
- Facebook groups for ADHD moms who do "cleaning swaps"

- Mutual aid groups that offer non-judgmental help

Give Yourself Permission to Start Over

If the system you made last month (or last year) isn't working anymore? Toss it.

Peel off the labels. Dump the bins. Start fresh.

Your house is not a museum. It's a living, breathing, messy, glorious space full of real humans. And sometimes it needs a reset, so do you.

Reality Check

- Are you avoiding a full reset because you think asking for help is "giving up"?

- Would you help a friend in your situation? Then you deserve that same kindness.

- Do you need support—or just permission?

Tiny Win Challenge

Text one person today and say, "Can you be my body double for a home reset?"

Or schedule a cleaner, ask for recommendations, or look up ADHD cleaning help in your area. The first step is just admitting: I need support. And that's a powerful move.

Bonus Tid Bits For Real Life Sanity

- Don't Aim for Pinterest. Aim for Peace. Pretty is optional. Functional is essential. Your systems don't need to impress, they just need to work for *you*.

Teach Your Kids the System (Then Expect to Repeat It 97 Times). If they don't know the system, they won't use it. If they forget the system, welcome to Groundhog Day parenting. Better yet, help them find their own desire paths!

- Your Home Should Work for You, Not the Other Way Around. If your organizing method makes life harder, it's not sacred, it's negotiable.

- A Label Isn't Permanent, It's Just a Suggestion. Masking tape is the ADHD mom's magic wand. Update it, move it, relabel it. No guilt.

- "Done" Is Better Than Perfect. Finished-ish beats ideal-but-never-happens every single time.

- Don't Sacrifice the Good for the Better. Of course it's better to recycle. But if that chili can is going to haunt your sink for two days while you dread rinsing it out, straight to the trash it goes. Mental health matters too.

- Your Kids Are Watching You Normalize Adaptability. Every system tweak is a parenting win. You're teaching them flexibility, problem-solving, and that it's okay to change your mind.

- Grace First. Then Trash Bags. Be kind to yourself. Then declutter with reckless abandon.

- System Breakdowns Are Just Data. If something keeps failing, it's not a sign you're a disaster, it's feedback. Pivot, tweak, and try again.

Reader Reflection Page

Because this isn't about perfection. It's about getting curious, staying honest, and building something that actually fits your life.

- What's one system you already use that actually works for your family?

- What's one part of your daily routine that's pure chaos (and might need a better system)?

- What's a "desire path" you've been ignoring? (Where do things naturally end up?)

- If I could wave a magic wand and fix one room or routine in my house, it would be:

- One system from this book I want to try this week:

- My family's weirdest clutter habit (and how I might work with it, not against it):

- A funny, real-life mess I no longer feel bad about:

Permission Slips

Print this. Cut it up. Tape them on your mirror. Or don't. I'm not the boss of you.

- I give myself permission to throw away the thing I "should" use but never do.

- I give myself permission to label the back of the couch "remote zone."

- I give myself permission to use disposable dishes if it keeps me from losing my mind.

- I give myself permission to stop chasing a perfect system and embrace a working one.

- I give myself permission to keep chargers in every room.

- I give myself permission to let my kids organize their stuff their way.

- I give myself permission to choose rhythm over rigor.

- I give myself permission to change my mind.

- I give myself permission to rest.

- I give myself permission to love my home, even when it's a mess.

Hot Mess Brain Hack:
Why Pen & Paper Checklists Actually Work

Writing things down by hand isn't just old-school—it's neuroscience. When you physically check something off a list:

- Your brain gets a dopamine hit.

That tiny "I did it!" rush is real—and addictive in the best way.

- It activates motor memory.

Writing helps your brain store the task better, so you're more likely to remember and repeat it.

- It creates a visual "ta-da!" list.

Your progress becomes tangible, not just mental. For ADHD brains, seeing success builds momentum.

- It quiets the noise.

Writing clears the mental clutter by getting swirling thoughts out of your head and onto the page. Boom—executive function booster.

So yes, printing the checklist at the end of this book and physically checking things off with a Sharpie or a glitter pen is not just satisfying—it's brain-friendly magic.

Hot Mess Hit List:
Common Chaos Zones to Conquer

A totally doable checklist for real-life homes (not museum displays)

Pick one. Tackle it. Repeat when the mood strikes.

The Usual Suspects:

- Kitchen counters (a.k.a. the clutter magnet)
- The laundry vortex (clean/dirty/???)
- Entryway drop zone (or lack thereof)
- Under the bathroom sink (aka expired-product purgatory)
- That one junk drawer you're scared of
- The floor of your closet
- The area behind/under/around the couch
- The top of your dresser (hello, emotional clutter)
- Nightstand catch-all zone
- The table that never gets used for eating
- "Put away later" basket that's now a lifestyle
- Sock drawer (no one said match them, just contain them)
- Kid artwork mountain
- Overflowing toy bins
- Paper piles (mail, school stuff, coupons from 2009)

- That tote of clothes to donate you've been ignoring
- The cabinet you open cautiously like it might explode
- Backpack/diaper bag/giant mom tote purge
- The fridge. You know why.

Books That Sparked Joy, Sanity, or Self-Acceptance

The Life-Changing Manga of Tidying Up by Marie Kondo
The only version of Marie Kondo's system that didn't make me feel personally attacked. It's cute, funny, and somehow got my kids to declutter without tears (mine or theirs).

Untamed by Glennon Doyle
A raw, electric reminder that you're allowed to take up space, trust your gut, and stop trying to make your life look like anyone else's. Especially the perfect moms on Instagram.

The Gifts of Imperfection by Brené Brown
The gospel of letting go of shame and expectations—and embracing your gloriously messy, wildly worthy self instead.

Daring Greatly by Brené Brown
Want to feel brave even when your kitchen's a disaster? This one's for you. Vulnerability is courage, and that includes showing up to your life (and your laundry) as-is.

How to Keep House While Drowning by KC Davis
The no-shame, no-expectation book that says, "You're not failing. You just need care tasks to work for you, not against you."

Your Brain's Not Broken by Tamara Rosier
Life-changing for ADHD brains who've internalized the idea that they're lazy or broken. Spoiler: you're neither.

Organizing Solutions for People with ADHD by Susan C. Pinsky
Skip the Pinterest aesthetics—this one gets right to the real-life hacks that make daily function doable.

Atomic Habits by James Clear

Even a hot mess mom can benefit from stacking tiny habits that stick. This one's pure science meets real life.

Author Bio

Genevieve West is a neurospicy mom of four, expert-level improviser, and creator of home systems that are just organized enough to keep things semi-sane. With 20+ years of experience in customer service, event coordination, and chaos management (read: parenting), she knows a thing or two about doing what works—even when it's not cute.

Her signature style combines humor, honesty, and actual help for overwhelmed moms who are sick of pretending they have it all together. She lives in Portland, Oregon, where the socks don't match, the remote has a labeled home, and love always comes before laundry.

978-1-300-22561-4
Imprint: Lulu.com

www.ingramcontent.com/pod-product-compliance
Lightning Source LLC
LaVergne TN
LVHW052258070426
835507LV00036B/3375